Which Way Is Detroit?

Herbert J. Strather

Which Way Is Detroit?
Copyright © 2024 by Herbert J. Strather

ISBN: 979-8894790800(sc)
ISBN: 979-8894790817(e)

All rights reserved. No part of this publication may be reproduced, distributed, or transmitted in any form or by any means, including photocopying, recording, or other electronic or mechanical methods, without the prior written permission of the publisher and/or the author, except in the case of brief quotations embodied in critical reviews and other noncommercial uses permitted by copyright law.

The views expressed in this book are solely those of the author and do not necessarily reflect the views of the publisher, and the publisher hereby disclaims any responsibility for them.

The Reading Glass Books
1-888-420-3050
www.readingglassbooks.com
fulfillment@readingglassbooks.com

TABLE OF CONTENTS

INTRODUCTION v

CHAPTER 1: The Questions You Should Ask Right Now… 1

CHAPTER 2: Hyper Growth areas Versus the Neighborhood 6

CHAPTER 3: Investing In Neighborhood Commercial Development 11
    Apartments 11
    Retail 13
    Net Leases 17
    Land 17

CHAPTER 4: Investing in Single Family Homes (1-4 units) 18
    3 C's 23
    Rental Properties 23

CHAPTER 5: What are the Financing Alternatives in Detroit? 25
    Land Contracts and Mortgages 25
    Capital Impact Partners 27
    Financial Institutions 33

CHAPTER 6: Buying Through Auctions? 38
    I. The Wayne County Sheriff Sales Auctions 39
    I. The Wayne County Property Tax Auction 40

CHAPTER 7: The 10 Biggest Mistakes Investors Make
and How to Avoid Them 42

CHAPTER 8: DETROIT ZIP CODES ~ "Hot Or Not." 45

CHAPTER 9: PROFORMA 72

CHAPTER 10: References Review 74
    Urban Property Management Companies 74
    Mortgage Brokers 75
    Real Estate Lawyers 75
    Service Providers 76

HERBERT J. STRATHER

DEVELOPING A NEW GENERATION OF REAL ESTATE ENTREPRENEURS.

Herbert J. Strather, a distinguished expert in urban real estate, presents the updated edition of **"Which Way Is Detroit,"** a comprehensive guide to maximizing investment opportunities in Detroit's dynamic real estate market. This edition provides fresh insights into the most promising areas for investment and offers detailed analysis of regions that deliver the greatest value for money. Additionally, it highlights unique financing tools available exclusively in Detroit, making it an indispensable resource for anyone looking to capitalize on these opportunities.

"Which Way Is Detroit" could have only been written by someone deeply rooted in Detroit, a true native dedicated to nurturing and cultivating the future leaders in real estate entrepreneurship. Herbert J. Strather is precisely that individual.

Strather embarked on his real estate journey at just eighteen, securing his first job as a real estate agent with the renowned Detroit-based Bowers Realty Company. Within a year, he rose to become the top sales agent not only at Bowers but also across the region. By 1974, after gaining expertise in real estate appraisals and income property brokerage, he established Strather & Associates, Inc., beginning to shape his significant footprint in the real estate sector through orchestrating complex transactions involving multi-dwelling units across the city.

Throughout the decades, Strather has collaborated with a host of influential partners, including former University of Michigan Regent, Nellie Varner. Together, they founded Strather & Varner, successfully closing over $250,000,000 in real estate deals from 1977 to 1990.

Since the 1990s, Strather & Associates, Inc. has facilitated over $2,000,000,000 in real estate transactions within the Detroit Metropolitan area. In 2004, they introduced "Woodbridge Estates," a 47-acre residential community that features single-family townhouses and condominiums, further cementing Strather's legacy in the Detroit real estate landscape.

"Woodbridge Estates"

A joint venture housing development, funded by Strather Trust and the Slavik Co. of Farmington Hills, is a sparkling example of Strather's determination and pride. The development has won numerous recognitions and reflects his dedication to Detroit. In 2014, Strather and partners received the 2014 Detroit Community Development Award for Excellence in Real Estate Development.

Strather also serves on a host of boards and committees, including the Detroit Economic Club but is most active in Optimist International, where he has personally built over 150 Optimist Clubs, making him the "Most Successful Builder of Civic Clubs in world history. In support of his commitment to Optimist International, Strather pledged and donated $1,000,000 to the Optimist Youth Foundation of Detroit which has provided more than 3,300 scholarships to deserving young people.

In 2008, Herbert J. Strather observed the devastating impact of the foreclosure crisis in Detroit, leading to widespread homelessness and helplessness. In response, he established Strather Academy (https://stratheracademy.com) to empower Detroiters with the knowledge to safeguard their homes. The academy teaches real estate strategies that not only advocate for homeownership but also equip students with the means to maintain, regain, or gracefully exit their homes with financial dignity.

As a dedicated teacher and coach, Strather has guided hundreds of students towards success in real estate. While his teachings reach students nationwide, his focus is intensely on Detroit, given its unique challenges and opportunities.

"WHICH WAY IS DETROIT" showcases Herbert J. Strather's deep commitment to mentoring those who seek to thrive in real estate and secure generational wealth, specifically in the city of Detroit.

Now the question is: **WHICH WAY IS DETROIT?**

Chapter 1

The Questions You Should Ask Right Now...

1.) Why is Detroit Getting All The Love?

2.) Why Should I Invest in Detroit?

3.) Why Detroit Now?

4.) Which Way is Detroit?

Psst! ... Here is your only answer.

"Detroit is The Top Choice for Smart Investing"

The Sun, Moon and the Stars have aligned to create perhaps the greatest investment opportunity of all times in Detroit post-bankruptcy and pandemic real estate. What is happening in the Motor City, which is known as the heartbeat of the world.

Detroit's current situation, deemed improbable by many experts, has been shaped by several key factors. These include the aftermath of the largest municipal bankruptcy in America, which left Detroit with $1,500,000,000 in cash and no debt, and well-intentioned, though potentially overzealous, government stimulus programs. Effective municipal management, the urban housing migration movement, supply and demand dynamics, and an abundance of raw housing inventory have also played crucial roles. Additionally, relatively low interest rates, a robust auto industry, a growing service sector, and the region's top status in philanthropy have collectively created an environment where an average but well-informed investor can achieve substantial wealth.

People all over the world are coming to Detroit by plane, train and cars to buy up Detroit's real estate in droves. While informed investors are making an unimaginable fortune, others are squatting to leap and getting cooked in the squat. Without question, the most important lesson is "Look before you leap. Don't try it alone. Take an expert with you."

This book is written to give guidance to Detroiters and everyone in the world willing to invest in Detroit. Without knowing the principles contained in this book, an investor would be foolish to plop down their hard-earned cash. There are stories of those who have taken a few hundred dollars and made thousands, and stories of those with millions invested; who still got wiped out.

If this publication accomplishes its goal, it becomes a win-win for all. Detroit communities can get reinvented, homeowners are spared loss of equity and/or disenfranchisement, investors are rewarded, and the author's legacy is fulfilled: "**To Help Bring Back the Magic To Detroit.**"

Buckle up, grab your favorite cup of coffee, and prepare for a rewarding journey of earning money while also rejuvenating the Heartbeat of the World!

THIS DECADE!

* Official Census Records

CONSIDER THIS:

Detroit's Investment Landscape: Post-Pandemic Resurgence and Strategic Opportunities

Throughout the Great Recession, Detroit faced severe challenges that were greater than those of nearly any other American city. The collapse of its iconic auto industry, coupled with political scandals and municipal bankruptcy, led to dramatically reduced real estate values. This created unprecedented investment opportunities, where quality properties in viable communities were obtainable at merely 50-70% of their pre-recession prices. Surprisingly, many of these opportunities still exist today in several neighborhoods.

Today, Detroit is a city of varied economic realities. While some areas are experiencing rapid growth with property values increasing by as much as 1,000%, other parts remain economically depressed, with properties still priced at 10-70% of their pre-recession values. This variation across the city highlights the different levels of economic recovery and development, presenting a range of investment potentials.

The COVID-19 pandemic further influenced Detroit's economic and demographic landscape. It highlighted the city's challenges but also its resilience and effective strategic responses.

Over 40,000 millennials have moved to Detroit this decade, attracted by the affordable cost of living and the opportunity to contribute to the city's revitalization. This influx is revitalizing the city's cultural and economic fabric and indicates a growing demand for housing and services.

Despite the global slowdown, Detroit's housing market shows remarkable recovery signs, with record-low real estate listings and rents in desirable neighborhoods returning to pre-recession levels. However, property prices remain significantly lower than their historical highs, suggesting a unique investment opportunity. This difference between rental incomes and property prices is primarily due to ongoing adjustments in supply and demand, influenced by the pandemic's economic impacts.

Strategic initiatives include leveraging Detroit down payment assistance programs and collaborating with Community Development Financial Institutions (CDFIs) that specialize in revitalization. These institutions are essential in providing the capital necessary for both new buyers and investors to engage in property purchases and renovations. Moreover, the city has emerged from bankruptcy with substantial cash reserves and minimal debt, supported by over $250,000,000 in commitments from Detroit's philanthropic sector aimed at enhancing targeted neighborhoods.

Conclusion: Detroit as a Prime Investment Destination Post-Pandemic

Detroit offers an unparalleled investment scenario today, combining quality real estate at low costs with robust support for rehabilitation. The city's management of pandemic challenges underscores its resilience and recovery capacity, making it an attractive destination for both new investors and seasoned developers. The strategic approach to urban investment not only promises substantial returns but also contributes to revitalizing a historic American city. Detroit's story of resurgence, particularly in the wake of recent global challenges, paints a vivid picture of a city ripe for investment, where strategic actions lead to real opportunities.

Typical street in northwest Detroit where a house that once sold for more than $100,000, now sells for a mere fraction of its former value.

Chapter 2

HYPER GROWTH AREAS VERSUS THE NEIGHBORHOOD

Detroit's rapidly evolving neighborhoods—including Downtown, Corktown, Midtown, and Lafayette Park, along with growth corridors extending from Woodward to Ferndale and Jefferson to Grosse Pointe—are attracting a vibrant new generation of residents who adore the city. While singles gravitate towards the bustling Downtown area, families find the surrounding neighborhoods more appealing. These regions are experiencing a surge in demand, driving up rents and property prices significantly.

The escalating interest in these prime areas is now beginning to overflow into adjacent neighborhoods. With this momentum, now presents a golden opportunity for real estate investments. Prospective investors might particularly consider new construction projects, especially if land can be acquired at reasonable prices. Current rental rates ranging from $2.00 to $3.50 per square foot make such developments feasible without the need for subsidies.

This period marks an ideal time to invest in these neighborhoods, with some areas demonstrating higher potential than others. Property values in these neighborhoods, although currently below their pre-covid levels by 50% to 70%, are poised for a rebound. There is ample inventory available for purchase and renovation, with sufficient demand to match.

Interestingly, while neighborhoods are revitalizing to their former states, Midtown—formerly known as the Cass Corridor and notorious as one of the city's most challenged areas for the past fifty years—is now experiencing unprecedented demand, the highest in Michigan. Adjacent to Wayne State University, a major expanding research institution, Midtown's transformation is particularly notable.

Investors are presented with several attractive options: the prime real estate of Greater Downtown, the major corridors, or the rebounding neighborhoods. Additional insights and detailed studies, such as those available from Detroit Future City (https://detroitfuturecity.com), offer further guidance for those interested in these dynamic markets.

A Declining Unemployment Rate Results In A More Favorable Job Market For Detroiters

Detroit Employment

Figure 1 below shows Detroit's unemployment rate alongside the city's labor force. Detroit's unemployment rate increased from 6.7% in Q2 2023 to 8.4% in Q3 2023 before declining to 7.6% in Q4 2023. That is roughly 1.0 percentage point higher than one year prior. However, this increase is primarily attributable to more Detroiters entering the labor force rather than losing jobs. In Q4 2023, Detroit's labor force reached 256,000 Detroiters, or 12,000 residents more than one year earlier.

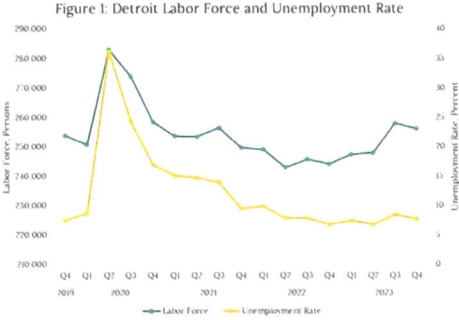

Source: Michigan Center for Data and Analytics, not seasonally adjusted

Additionally, the state's unemployment rate ticked up from 4.0% in Q3 2023 to 4.1% in Q4 2023, as Michiganders continued to enter the workforce. In fact, just over 5,044,700 Michiganders were in the state's labor force in Q4 2023, which is the highest labor force count that the state has seen since Q2 2004.

Just as the housing market in Detroit is the best place to invest, unemployment is falling below pre-recession levels. The city is anchored by large employers in:

- The Health industry (Henry Ford Health and Detroit Medical Center)
- The Auto industry (GM, Ford, Chrysler-Fiat)
- The Financial industry (Quicken Loans, Deloitte, Amazon)
- The Casino industry that Mr. Strather helped create.

Detroit is also becoming an innovation center thriving with tech incubators and residences for budding entrepreneurs and startups.

Detroit Population Measures Are Rebounding With Shifting Composition

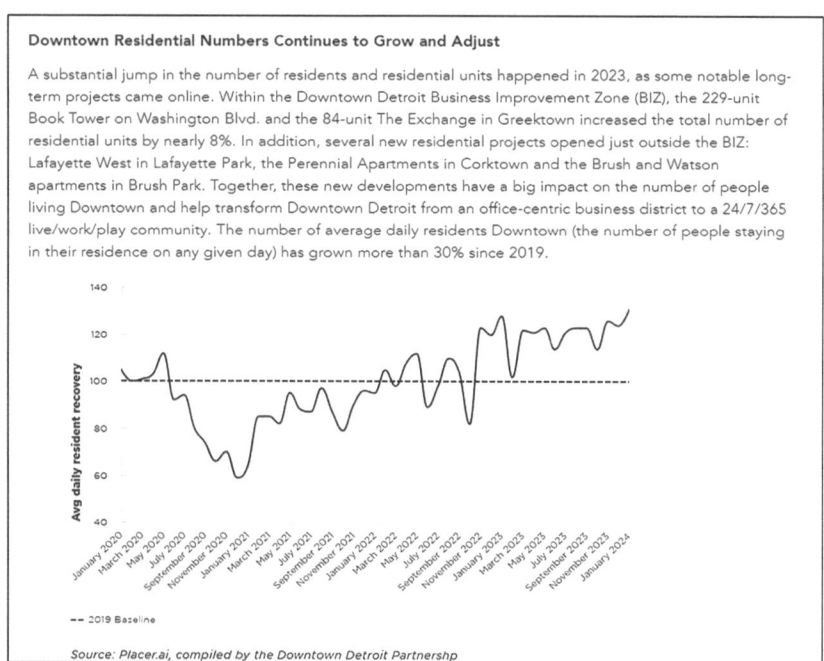

The Downtown population has grown, surpassing pre-recession volumes and is expected to increase as new residential property becomes available.

Millennials comprise the largest demographic, making up 32% of the downtown area population ~ signaling an influx of art, culture, and technological innovation.

The diverse composition of age groups, each possessing unique skills, presents opportunities for growth and development in the real estate industry, benefiting both new and established investors and developers.

Building Permits Issued in Growth Communities Are A Promising Sign

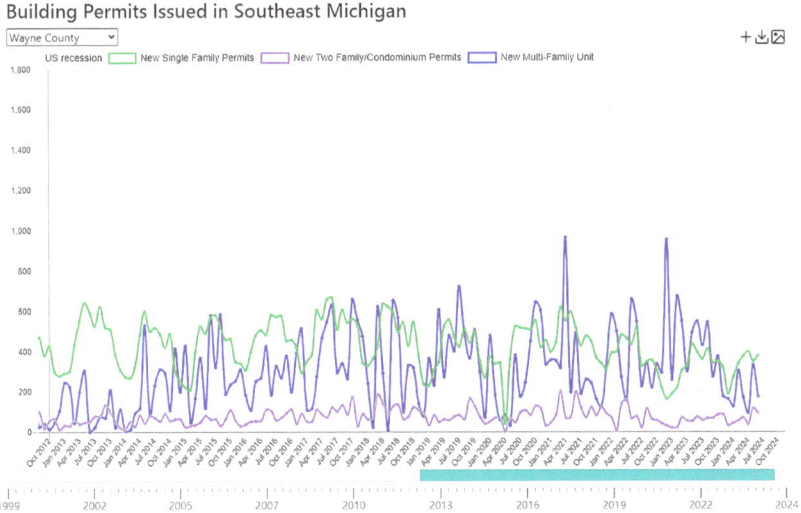

The rise of permits are illustrated by the clustering effect on the map.

Neighborhoods along the Jefferson and Woodward corridors have noticeable clustering, corresponding with the advent of the M-1 rail, building of the new sports facilities and the proximity to Belle Isle and Grosse Pointe.

Rising numbers of building permits not only signify home construction improvement, but also economic and socio-cultural activity, as demonstrated in the Midtown area. (Museums, restaurants, new houses and condos).

Detroit's Neighborhoods Could Be Summarized Into Four Different Categories

As of 2024, upper-class, high-end communities such as Palmer Woods, University District, Rosedale Park, and Indian Village have not only recovered from the 2008 financial downturn but have also seen appreciable growth in property values. These neighborhoods continue to attract significant interest due to their historic appeal and robust community investments, potentially exceeding previous peak valuations.

Solid Middle-Class Communities in Northwest and Northeast Detroit, Including Aviation Subdivision: These areas have seen a moderate recovery in property values, with demand currently outpacing the available supply. This imbalance suggests potential for notable appreciation in property values over the next few years.

Lower and Lower-Middle Income Communities Such as Wyoming/Grand River and Whittier/Kelly: While these neighborhoods have experienced a slower recovery rate, they offer attractive opportunities for investors, characterized by relatively high Capitalization Rates. This makes them appealing for those seeking higher returns on investment.

Greater Downtown Area, Including Midtown, Lafayette Park, and the Jefferson and Woodward Corridors: This region is experiencing significant growth, with property values showing substantial increases compared to a decade ago. The surge in development and investment continues to transform these areas into high-demand real estate markets."

CHAPTER 3

INVESTING IN NEIGHBORHOOD COMMERCIAL DEVELOPMENT

APARTMENTS

Apartments are a winner. During the recession Detroit lost many apartment buildings resulting in a shortage of affordable units. This is evidenced by the fact that owners of quality apartment units are now full. This is in stark contrast to 2009 - 2011 when Detroit experienced a 20-30% vacancy and collection factor.

As stated earlier, since the recession some rental rates have increased for $1.00-1.30 Per Sq. Ft. to more than $3.00 Per Sq. Ft. in the Hyper-Growth communities and main growth corridors. This means that you can renovate or build brand new units without subsidies.

The Cap Rate in these areas have gone from 10-12% to around 6-10%. I predict over the next couple of years Detroit will explode with new apartments to meet the demand. There is also great upside in purchasing and rehabbing modern apartment buildings especially areas in Northwest Detroit.

Properties in good areas that need rehab can be bought for $35,000 - $50,000 per unit, add $5,000 per unit for upgrades and replacements, and you have a great investment. Consider this - apartments are renting for about $1.50 per square foot, per month in NW Detroit. So, a 700 sq. ft. unit rents annually for $12,000 annually Deduct $5,000 for expenses and vacancy/collection and you have somewhere around a $6,000 per unit Net Operating Income. That equates to 10-11%.

Where else in the world can you get a healthy cap rate like Detroit's? Cap rates in Florida, California, Toronto and New York are 2-5%. Now is a great time to invest in the City of Detroit.

Since the recession, Detroit's rental market has undergone significant changes, showing a consistent upward trend in rental prices. In neighborhoods like Lafayette Park, the average rent for a one-bedroom apartment has reached approximately $1,527 per month by 2024. This reflects a broader trend across the city, where rental costs have been rising due to increased demand and a revitalized interest in urban living. This information underscores the evolving dynamics of Detroit's housing market, highlighting the city's recovery and growth in the post-recession era. More info can be found here: https://www.rent.com.

Capitalization rates (Cap Rates) in these regions have adjusted from historical highs of 10-12% to more stabilized figures around 6-8%, reflecting a maturing market that still offers substantial growth potential. Predictions suggest that Detroit will see a surge in apartment development in the coming years to meet growing demand, particularly in neighborhoods like Northwest Detroit, where there is significant potential for rehabilitating and modernizing apartment buildings. Further insights are available here: https://www.point2homes.com.

Investment opportunities in Detroit remain robust, with the potential for strong returns on investments in properties requiring rehabilitation, given the current rental rates and market conditions. This presents a favorable investment landscape compared to other major urban markets like Florida, California, Toronto, and New York, where Cap Rates typically range from 2-5%. A comprehensive overview of this can be explored at: https://www.rentdata.org.

In summary, Detroit's real estate market offers compelling opportunities for investors, underpinned by rising rental rates and a conducive economic environment for property development and rehabilitation.

RETAIL

Detroit is starving for more retail, and it is coming. The "D" is one of the only cities in the USA that does not have plenty of national, sit-down restaurants where you can buy a drink and get a great meal. I am talking about Friday's, Red Lobster, Applebee's, etc. Additionally, many of the big boxes do not exist in Detroit. For example, there are no Walmart's in the city. What's interesting, is whenever a new store opens in Detroit it becomes the number one store in the retailer's portfolio.

So, why don't more retailers come to Detroit? The answer is (1) fear of the unknown and (2) several horror stories. Yes, crime is higher, so security costs are more. However, rents are reasonable, and sales are off the hook. These are the reasons why companies like Rainbow, Meijer and Foreman Mills have done great.

Home Depot has done very well in the city also, anchoring the store on 7-Mile and Meyers in NW Detroit. The new location of Forman Mills in the Tower Center and Home Depot are accomplishments from the author of this book, Herbert J. Strather.

One of the top secrets to success in retailing is joint venturing with local churches to hire employees. Let them do the hiring or screening for you, while putting the fear of God in their hearts, ultimately reducing shrinkage. Now is a great time to locate quality retail in neighborhoods that are bouncing back. The best retail for Detroit now is national restaurants and big boxes.

Stores surrounding Detroit have some of the highest sales volume nationally, think what would happen if more stores were in Detroit instead of the suburbs.

Downtown Detroit is currently a hotspot for several major commercial construction projects that are set to redefine the cityscape. Some of the key developments include:

1. **Hudson's Site Development**: This massive project is transforming the historic site of the former Hudson's Department Store into a multi-use complex featuring office spaces, residential units, a hotel, and retail areas. The project includes the construction of a significant new addition to Detroit's skyline with a tower expected to reach a height of 685 feet, making it one of the tallest buildings in the state upon completion in 2024.

2. **The Ralph C. Wilson Centennial Park**: An ambitious project that is turning a former industrial site along the Detroit riverfront into a 22-acre public park. This development aims to provide extensive green space, recreational facilities, and event venues to boost community engagement and urban renewal.

3. **Big Sean's Cinema Venture**: In partnership with Emagine Entertainment, Detroit native rapper Big Sean is planning to open a new movie theater in the city. This venue is expected to enhance the local entertainment scene significantly.

4. **Target's Midtown Debut**: Target is set to open a new 32,000-square-foot store in Midtown, marking its return to Detroit with a smaller-format store tailored to urban settings. This development is anticipated to add a significant retail boost to the area.

5. **Residential and Hotel Developments**: Several new towers and residential developments are underway, including a new residential tower on the Joe Louis Arena site almost completed and a hotel near the convention center, which will add considerable accommodation spaces to the city's core.

These projects reflect a broader trend of investment and development in Detroit, aimed at revitalizing the downtown area and making it a more vibrant, livable, and economically robust part of the city.

The ongoing commercial developments in downtown Detroit not only offer direct investment opportunities but also play a pivotal role in revitalizing inner-city areas and enhancing local economic activities. Here's how these projects are shaping both downtown and inner-city investment landscapes:

1. **Economic Stimulation**: Large projects such as the Hudson's site redevelopment and the introduction of a Target store in Midtown lead to increased economic activity that can ripple through the inner city. This creates opportunities for both large and small businesses to open or expand, leveraging the increased foot traffic and improved infrastructure.

2. **Property Value Appreciation**: As major developments progress, property values in surrounding inner-city areas are likely to rise. This trend presents lucrative opportunities for real estate investors to acquire properties for commercial, residential, or mixed-use developments, potentially yielding high returns as the areas continue to develop.

3. **Job Creation**: The construction phase and operational needs of these developments generate numerous jobs, which helps to lower unemployment rates in the inner city. With more residents employed, there's an increase in disposable income and consumer spending within the community, supporting local businesses and encouraging further investments.

4. **Infrastructure Improvements**: Significant projects often come with necessary upgrades to local infrastructure, such as enhanced roads, public transport, and utilities. These improvements make the inner-city areas more accessible and attractive for new businesses and residents, fostering a more dynamic urban environment conducive to further investments.

5. **Community Development and Quality of Life**: Projects like the Ralph C. Wilson Centennial Park and the Joe Louis Greenway focus on creating public spaces that enhance community well-being. These developments not only make the inner-city areas more desirable but also support a community-focused approach to urban development, attracting more residents and businesses who value these qualities.

6. **Cultural and Environmental Enhancements**: With developments like Big Sean's cinema venture and various public parks, there's a strong focus on enriching the cultural landscape and maintaining environmental sustainability. These aspects attract a diverse population and encourage businesses that align with these values, thereby creating a vibrant, sustainable urban community.

These ongoing developments signify a broader trend of investment and revitalization efforts in Detroit, aimed at transforming both the economic landscape and the quality of life for its residents. By capitalizing on these opportunities, local investors can play a significant role in shaping Detroit's future as a flourishing urban center.

NET LEASES

Net leases, where tenants are responsible for paying some or all of the property expenses in addition to rent, are generally a sound investment regardless of location. In Detroit, such leases are typically held by creditworthy tenants in sectors like drug stores, auto parts stores, and certain restaurants. These businesses, which often boast stable sales, present solid investment opportunities that vary depending on the neighborhood.

LAND

Purchasing land can be a winner but you must know where to buy it. Perhaps the best plan would be to study the growth corridors and buy just beyond them. Consider this -- Detroit Riverfront is golden, so travel one to two miles north of the water and buy dirt. Sooner or later the good life will catch up to you. I bet; you can buy lots for $200-$1,000 all day long. Just buy enough to make a difference when a development opportunity comes around.

CHAPTER 4

INVESTING IN SINGLE FAMILY HOMES (1-4 UNITS)

THE FIVE - F's:

    1.) FINDING (*Taking control of*)

    2.) FUNDING (*Cash transactions*)

    3.) FINANCING (*OPM or your credit*)

    4.) FIXING (*Tradesmen skills*)

    5.) FLIPPING (*the easy part, finding a buyer*)

FINDING

First you must determine what you want, then focus on it. For local investors, buy where you live, work, play or pray. For those living outside of **Detroit** do not try it home alone, take your **A-Team** with you. It's ok to do research online and find deals, but outside investors must have boots on the ground and know the psychographics of the neighborhood. At the end of this guide, is a partial list of firms and individuals with solid reputations that do business in **Detroit**.

Now about finding deals… **Deals in the "D"** are everywhere. On almost every street there is usually at least one opportunity. You can look at a property by driving around (**blitzing**) or by using technology. Google maps being a prime example.

With today's technology you can find **Deals in Detroit** from anywhere in the world; all you need is a local partner or professional to verify the situation. This can best be done with persons that know the lay of the land and the future projected psychographics of the neighborhoods (the boots on the ground person). The novice investor should stick with the good stuff. On almost every block, you will find at least one vacant house. I would say look for the best blocks with the best neighbors and buy there.

Do not buy on blocks with lots of **vacant houses** unless you have a game plan for the entire block. Buy a property you can rent to a single mom where she would feel safe raising her children. Remember there are plenty of scrapers and thieves waiting to rip off property owners. Properties in good areas are less likely to be ripped off because the neighbors/homeowners are much more active and sensitive.

The other F's are also very important, but everything starts with finding the right deal. For some investors, the best play is to purchase a deal already done with a tenant or homeowner.

Consider these websites for finding good deals in Detroit;

<https://buildingdetroit.org/>
<https://www.hudhomesusa.org/landing.html>
<https://www.mls.com>
<https://stratheracademy.com>
<https://www.legalnews.com>

P.S. Nothing Beats Blitzing with is getting into your car and driving around finding deals you want to acquire

FUNDING

Cash is highly valued in the marketplace due to its speed and the lack of liquidity in certain neighborhoods. Auctions are the optimal venue for cash transactions. Most vacant residential real estate deals require a cash infusion beyond the purchase price to make the property move-in ready or financeable. The majority of transactions in the city involve all-cash deals, primarily from investors outside Detroit.

FINANCING

Many major banks are not currently offering mortgages to investors; however, there are several other lenders that will. Check in the reference section in this book.

FIXING

Many owners of vacant homes are willing to sell to contractors. They should use a deed or Land Contract held in escrow. After the contractor finishes the work to the owner's satisfaction, they get ownership. The owner might provide materials and accept 75% of the contractor's labor as the down payment. Got it?

FLIPPING

Using someone else's money to finance a real estate deal, commonly referred to as "other people's money" (OPM), is a strategy that many investors use to minimize their own risk and increase their potential return on investment. Here are a few ways to do it:

1. **Private Money Lenders:**
   - **Friends and Family**: Borrowing money from friends or family can be a quick way to get the funds you need. Ensure that terms are clearly defined to avoid misunderstandings.
   - **Private Investors**: These are individuals who invest their money in real estate deals in exchange for a return on their investment. They can be found through networking events, real estate investment groups, or online platforms.

2. **Hard Money Lenders:**
   - These are typically private lenders or companies that provide short-term loans secured by real estate. Hard money loans usually have higher interest rates but can be a good option for quick funding.

3. **Partnerships:**
   - Partnering with other investors who can provide the necessary capital can be a beneficial arrangement. In return, you can offer your expertise, a share of the profits, or a combination of both.

4. **Seller Financing:**
   - Sometimes, sellers are willing to finance part or all of the sale price. This means you make payments directly to the seller instead of getting a traditional mortgage.

5. **Wholesaling:**
   - In this strategy, you find a property, get it under contract, and then sell the contract to another investor for a fee. This way, you don't need to actually purchase the property yourself.

6. **Crowdfunding:**
   - Real estate crowdfunding platforms allow you to pool money from multiple investors to finance a property. This can be an effective way to raise capital without relying on a single source.

7. **Joint Ventures:**
   - Form a joint venture with another investor or a group of investors where each party contributes different resources, such as capital, skills, or properties.

Example: If you find a property you want to flip, you could enter into an agreement with a private investor who provides the purchase money. You do the work to flip the property, and then you both share the profits according to the terms agreed upon. The private investor could have a normal fixed return with equity sharing in the form of a Participating Promissory Note

Steps to Using Someone Else's Money:

1. **Identify the Property**: Find a profitable real estate deal.

2. **Create a Business Plan**: Detail the investment opportunity, including costs, potential profits, timelines, and risks.

3. **Pitch to Investors**: Present your plan to potential investors, highlighting the benefits and how they will get a return on their investment.

4. **Agree on Terms**: Negotiate and agree on the terms of the

investment, including the percentage of profits, repayment terms, and responsibilities.

5. **Secure the Agreement**: Formalize the agreement in writing to protect all parties involved.

6. **Execute the Deal**: Use the funds to purchase and renovate the property, then sell or rent it as planned.

7. **Return on Investment**: Share the profits with your investors according to the agreed terms.

By leveraging other people's money, you can increase your buying power and potential returns while spreading the risk. Always ensure clear agreements and transparent communication to maintain trust and protect all parties involved.

Remember, however you are giving up future profits because values are depressed. The smart money says rent now and sell later. If you are going to flip - use LLCs with one asset – the property. LLCs give you the option to either deed the property to the new owner or assign the membership interest.

3 C'S

In order to succeed in real estate in the **"D"** or any other place, you must provide one of the 3 C's: Cash, Credit, Collateral Or Cell phone, Computer, Car with gas along with a big-time commitment!

RENTAL PROPERTIES

The supply, demand and cost including interest rates over the last five years have caused rents to spike 20% for new move-ins. However, most landlords have not adjusted their rents 20% because they would wipe out their buildings. Interestingly however appraisers base value on market rate rents and not on current rents. This means there's a lot of built-up equity in apartments and if structured properly you could fully finance almost any apartment in Detroit without putting down any equity especially since the cap rates are greater than the debt rates (constants).

The other thing that's very important to remember is in a marketplace like Detroit where there's a tremendous amount of buoyancy, lenders and appraisers are most influenced by the purchase agreement. So many smart investors offer a higher price and take credits back for closing costs or repairs. This methodology not only helps the investor come up with less cash to close if any, it also stabilizes values in the community. This works best when buying property directly adjacent to a rapidly appreciating community like Bagley that is located adjacent to the University of Detroit community.

CHAPTER 5

WHAT ARE THE FINANCING ALTERNATIVES IN DETROIT?

Land Contracts and Mortgages

Financing investment real estate under $50,000 presents a problem. Many properties in Detroit as of the end of 2018 are under $50,000. The lenders of choice are CDFIs, private money, Credit Unions and a small handful of banks.

The banks surely have no appetite for investment in real estate, in fact many are prohibited from making loans on investments of real estate; but thank God for others.

Credit Unions

Credit unions' purposes are to serve its members and are not driven by profits alone. Most credit unions do not have the staff to underwrite mortgages, especially commercial transactions, so they rely on Credit Union Service Corporations (CUSCs). These entities are consortiums of several credit unions that syndicate loans.

The two CUSCs in Michigan are "Commercial Alliance" and "Michigan Business Connect". They want standard vanilla loans, meaning no creative turnaround projects. They do not fund huge deals, with sums around $25,000,000. Their limits are usually around $1,000,000-$5,000,000 and they want good credit.

Contact them at:

Mortgage Center

1-800-353-4449

Member First

1-866-898-1818

Commercial Alliance

1-800-518-4096

Michigan Business Connection

1-734-662-0614

Community Development Financing Institutions

For commercial loans, we have entities called Community Development Financing Institutions (CDFIs) and there are several in Detroit. They are the best vehicle for commercial deals. As a thought exercise, consider this, they can finance up to 90% loan to value with a 110% Debt Coverage Ratio. Wow! Which way are the CDFIs?

Some of the more popular CDFIs are:

Capital Impact Partners

A mission driven community development financial institution, Capital Impact Partners are headquartered in Arlington, VA, Oakland, CA and Detroit, MI. They also have staff located in key regions across the country to better service your needs. If you have a project that creates social impact, we want to partner with you.

Headquarters	**West Coast**	**Midwest**
1400 Crystal Drive Suite 500 Arlington, VA 22202	360 22nd Street Suite 320 Oakland, CA 94612	2990 West Grand Boulevard Suite M-15 Detroit, MI 48202
Phone: (703) 647-2300	Phone: (510) 496-2222	Phone: (313) 230-1116
Fax: (703) 647-3490	Fax: (510) 496-0404	

Corporation for Supportive Housing

A Mission to advance housing solutions that deliver three powerful outcomes: 1) Improve lives for the most vulnerable people. 2) Maximize public resources. 3) Maximize strong, healthy communities across the country.

440 Burroughs St., Suite 523 Detroit, MI 48202

Phone: 313-209-6949

Fax: 313-254-4179

Local Initiatives Support Corporations
LISC

Is one of the largest organizations supporting projects to revitalize communities and bring greater economic opportunity to residents. These include more affordable housing, better schools, safer streets, growing businesses and programs that improve the financial outlook of people. LISC also provides the capital, strategy and know-how to get this done.

>600 Woodward Ave., Suite 1600
>Detroit, MI 48226
>
>(313) 265-2819

IFF

A mission-driven lender, real estate consultant and developer that helps communities thrive. IFF brings a deep sense of purpose and brand perspective to low-income communities and people with disabilities across the Midwest. Non- Profits only.

>3011 W. Grand Blvd.
>Suite 1715
>Detroit, MI 48202
>313-309-7825

Invest Detroit

Is a catalyst for economic growth managing a variety of targeted funds? We finance and support business development, commercial real estate, entrepreneurs, and high-tech companies in Detroit and the region. We collaborate with the public, private, and philanthropic sectors to create jobs, density, sustainability, and opportunity for underserved communities and markets.

600 Renaissance Center, Suite 1710	Woodward Willis office location:
Detroit, Michigan 48243-1802	4219 Woodward Avenue
Info@investdetroit.com	Detroit, Michigan 48201
p: 313-259-6368	
f: 313-259-6393	

Freddie Mac has funding in Detroit with their small loan program, which max out at $5,000,000 per project. It starts at $1,000,000.

Earlier in the decade, some mortgage lenders and hedge funds did not want Detroit real estate in their portfolio, especially if they were trying to sell shares to both public and institutions. Of course, that mindset has changed.

For residential homeownership only, there is fabulous financing in the "D" with these lenders!

NACA

The **Neighborhood Assistance Corporation of America** is a national affordable lending program that provides mortgages for low - and moderate-income families. It was created in a settlement with Bank of America and CITI-Corp for their abusive lending practices. As a result, they have a spectacular program. Here are the highlights:

- No down payment, 100% financing up to the full- After Repair Value (ARV).
- Will loan 10% over and above the ARV for improvements.
- 30-year financing with rates .25% less than FHA with no mortgage insurance.
- No lender closing costs other than property tax & insurance escrows.
- Based on credit history and 'NOT' credit scores.
- Uses all sources of income including, alimony, SSI, Section 8 Certificates (Housing Choice Vouchers).
- Interest Rate Buy Down: (example) 1% of the loan amount (also called one point) reduces the interest rate by .025% for a 30-year loan.

If this is not good enough, consider that at the end of last year NACA had hundreds of buyers in the pipeline looking for homes.

Acquire-- Strather Academy Home Study Course: "Leveraging Real Estate", it speaks for itself @ (www.stratheracademy.com)

Strategic Neighborhood Fund

This is a very exciting time in Detroit – just a few years after Detroit's bankruptcy the city has rebounded; now real estate investors around the world are focused on Detroit. On December 10, 2018 an announcement was made by City officials that 7 corporations invested $35,000,000 dollars in the form of business development, single-family and affordable housing, parks and green space, as well as improvements to streetscapes in an initiative called the **Strategic Neighborhood Fund**. One-half of the money went to the **Affordable Housing Leverage Fund** which has leveraged the investment into hundreds of millions of dollars in public private investment for affordable multi-family projects. Wow!!

Financing Options For Acquiring Real Estate:

1. **Hard Money Loans:** Short-term loans secured by real estate, often used by investors for quick financing. They have higher interest rates and shorter repayment periods compared to conventional loans.

2. **Home Equity Line of Credit (HELOC):** A loan in which the lender agrees to lend a maximum amount within an agreed period, where the collateral is the borrower's equity in their home.

3. **Seller Financing:** A real estate agreement where the seller handles the mortgage process instead of a financial institution. The buyer makes payments directly to the seller.

4. **Federal Housing Administration (FHA) Loans:** Government-backed loans that make it easier for homebuyers to qualify for a mortgage, especially those with lower credit scores or smaller down payments.

5. **Cash-Out Refinance:** Replacing an existing mortgage with a new one that is larger than the amount owed on the original

loan, allowing the borrower to take the difference in cash.

6. **Crowdfunding:** Raising small amounts of money from a large number of people, typically via the internet, to finance a real estate project or purchase.

7. **Veterans United Home Loans:** Mortgage loans specifically designed for veterans, active-duty military members, and their families, often with favorable terms like zero down payment.

8. **Commercial Mortgage-Backed Securities (CMBS) Loans:** Loans secured by commercial properties that are pooled together and sold as bonds to investors.

9. **Lease Options:** A lease agreement that gives the tenant the option to purchase the property at the end of the lease period.

10. **Life Insurance Policy Loans:** Borrowing against the cash value of a life insurance policy.

11. **Real Estate Crowdfunding:** Using crowdfunding to pool money from multiple investors to purchase or develop real estate properties.

12. **Borrowing from Parents:** Obtaining a loan from family members, typically with more flexible terms than traditional loans.

13. **Construction Loans:** Short-term loans used to finance the building of a property, which are usually converted into a permanent mortgage once the construction is completed.

14. **Lease Agreements:** Contracts between a landlord and tenant outlining the terms under which the tenant can occupy and use the property.

15. **Owner Financing:** A transaction where the seller of the property finances the purchase for the buyer, allowing them to make payments directly to the seller over time.

16. **Personal Property Loans:** Loans that are secured by personal property other than real estate, such as vehicles or equipment.

17. **Portfolio Loans:** Loans that a lender holds in its own portfolio instead of selling them on the secondary market, often allowing for more flexible terms.

18. **Conventional Loans:** Mortgage loans that are not insured or guaranteed by the government, typically offered by private lenders.

19. **Personal Loans:** Unsecured loans that can be used for various purposes, including real estate investments, with repayment terms based on the borrower's creditworthiness.

20. **Private Money Loans:** Loans provided by private individuals or companies rather than traditional banks or credit unions, often used for real estate investments.

21. **Commercial Loans:** Loans intended for commercial purposes, such as purchasing business real estate or financing business operations.

22. **Balloon and Piggyback Loans:**
    - Balloon Loans: Loans that have small monthly payments and a large payment due at the end of the term.
    - Piggyback Loans: Second mortgages taken out at the same time as the first mortgage to avoid paying private mortgage insurance.

23. **Economic Development Grants:** Non-repayable funds provided by governments or organizations to support economic growth, which can include real estate projects.

24. **Private Loans:** Loans from private individuals or entities, which can be more flexible than traditional financing options but may come with higher interest rates.

Financial Institutions

Commercial Alliance

Overview: Commercial Alliance specializes in providing commercial loans through credit unions, focusing on standard loans ranging from $1,000,000 to $5,000,000. They do not typically fund high-risk turnaround projects.

Contact Information:

- **Phone:** 1-800-518-4096
- **Website:** https://www.commercialalliance.com
- **Address:** 30400 Telegraph Rd Suite 410, Bingham Farms, MI 48025

Michigan Business Connection

Overview: Michigan Business Connection (MBC) supports small and medium-sized businesses by underwriting and originating commercial loans for financial institutions. They primarily serve Michigan credit unions and their members, managing a portfolio of over $1.5 billion in business loans.

Contact Information:

- **Phone:** 1-866-642-4287
- **Fax:** 1-734-662-2465
- **Email:** info@mbcloans.biz
- **Website:** https://www.mbcloans.biz
- **Address:** 2200 Commonwealth Blvd, Suite 200, Ann Arbor, MI 48105

Community Development Financial Institutions (CDFIs)

CDFIs play a crucial role in financing commercial real estate in Detroit, often providing up to 90% loan-to-value with a 110% Debt Coverage Ratio.

Capital Impact Partners

Overview: Capital Impact Partners focuses on projects that create social impact, providing substantial support for community development initiatives.

Contact Information:

- **Detroit Office:** 2990 West Grand Boulevard, Suite M-15, Detroit, MI 48202
- **Phone:** (313) 230-1116
- **Website:** https://www.capitalimpact.org

Headquarters:

- **Address:** 1400 Crystal Drive, Suite 500, Arlington, VA 22202
- **Phone:** (703) 647-2300
- **Fax:** (703) 647-3490

West Coast Office:

- **Address:** 360 22nd Street, Suite 320, Oakland, CA 94612
- **Phone:** (510) 496-2222
- **Fax:** (510) 496-0404

Corporation for Supportive Housing (CSH)

Overview: CSH improves lives through housing solutions, supporting vulnerable populations and promoting healthy communities.

Contact Information:

- **Address:** 440 Burroughs St., Suite 523, Detroit, MI 48202
- **Phone:** (313) 209-6949
- **Fax:** (313) 254-4179
- **Website:** https://www.capitalimpact.org

Local Initiatives Support Corporation (LISC)

Overview: LISC provides financial and strategic support for projects enhancing community development, including affordable housing and economic revitalization.

Contact Information:

- **Address:** 600 Woodward Ave., Suite 1600, Detroit, MI 48226
- **Phone:** (313) 265-2819
- **Website:** https://www.lisc.org

IFF

Overview: IFF is a mission-driven lender focused on supporting non-profits and low-income communities, providing loans, real estate consulting, and development services.

Contact Information:

- **Address:** 3011 W. Grand Blvd., Suite 1715, Detroit, MI 48202
- **Phone:** (313) 309-7825
- **Website:** https://www.iff.org

Invest Detroit

Overview: Invest Detroit manages various funds to support economic growth, business development, and real estate projects, focusing on job creation and community sustainability.

Contact Information:

- **Main Office:** 600 Renaissance Center, Suite 1710, Detroit, MI 48243
- **Phone:** (313) 259-6368
- **Fax:** (313) 259-6393
- **Email:** info@investdetroit.com
- **Website:** https://www.investdetroit.com

Woodward Willis Office:

- **Address:** 4219 Woodward Avenue, Detroit, MI 48201

NACA (Neighborhood Assistance Corporation of America)

Overview: NACA offers affordable lending programs with no down payment, 100% financing up to the After-Repair Value, and below-market interest rates, prioritizing low- and moderate-income families.

Key Features:

- **No down payment**
- **No closing costs or fees**
- **No private mortgage insurance (PMI)**

- **Below-market fixed interest rates**
- **Flexible borrower qualification guidelines**
- **Comprehensive home buyer education and counseling**

Contact Information:
- **Website:** https://www.naca.com
- **Phone:** 1-425-602-6222 (National Office)
- **Address:** Check the NACA website: https://www.naca.com for local office addresses and contact details.

Strategic Neighborhood Fund

Overview: Launched by the City of Detroit, this fund supports business development, affordable housing, and community improvements. Corporate investments have leveraged significant public-private partnerships to boost neighborhood revitalization.

Contact Information:
- **Website:** https://detroitmi.gov

For more information and interactive detailed maps go to:

City of Detroit, Department of Neighborhoods:
https://detroitmi.gov

We especially appreciate the Companies listed below who are committed to Detroit. These are the Companies that are helping to make it happen.

CHAPTER 6

BUYING THROUGH AUCTIONS?

A mention of any guide to buying in Detroit would not be complete without talking about the **2** (two) major Wayne County Auctions.

In order to have a successful Auction Bidding outcome you need to develop an underwriting routine that is consistent. You **must** underwrite everything relative to the acquisition, including the occupants, the real estate, the taxes, the utilities and the community.

Learning by experience, trial and error is the most expensive way to learn.

I. The Wayne County Sheriff Sales Auctions

Held **weekly** on the 13th floor of the Coleman A. Young Municipal Center building. Located at: Two Woodward Ave in downtown

Detroit. The bidding begins at 11:00 am. Approximate 50 parcels are auctioned at a time, but the average of only about 25-30% are sold. Some of the properties start at $5,000 or less, even if the mortgage balance is $50,000 or more.

Many of the homes are occupied and the owners have **redemption rights** ranging from three months to one year. Here you must be very, very careful. 1. Sometimes the foreclosures are 2nd mortgages or liens or even delinquent. 2. Homeowners sometimes owe Association dues. 3. Sheriff Sale Properties can also have delinquent property taxes and gigantic water bills.

You **MUST** do your research and homework because there are **no refunds** at Wayne County Sheriff Sale Auctions.

II. The Wayne County Property Tax Auction

This is the Super Bowl of auctions with thousands of parcels being auctioned off annually for pennies on the dollar. The numbers, however, have been changing drastically; for example, prior to 2016, there were more than twenty thousand parcels auctioned off. There were more than twenty thousand that qualified, but twenty thousand was the most the system could handle in the time allocated. In 2016, the parcels being auctioned shrank to seventeen thousand, and in 2018, it had dwindled down to only seven thousand. Now in 2024 the number is closer to 2,000. The prices have also dramatically increased. The prospects for great prices at the auction are also diminishing but are still good if you do thorough research & underwriting. **Don't Bid Blind.**

The minimum deposits to bid have also changed. Prior to 2015, a deposit of $500 was required. Starting in 2015, the game changed. Bidders must now deposit $2,500 to bid for a single parcel even if they only want to bid up to $1,000. The successful bidder also must pay the current taxes at the time they pay for the bid. In order to bid on multiple properties, bidders need a deposit of $10,000.

There are essentially two (2) opportunities to bid at the Wayne County Tax Auction.

1.) One opportunity occurs in September whereas the minimum bid starts at the full amount of taxes owed.

2.) The second opportunity is November whereas the bid starts at $500.

The strategic auction guide "***Bidding On A Prayer***" is now available at https://stratheracademy.com.

Overall, the Wayne County Auctions have become much more competitive; apparently, investors around the world have heard about Wayne County Auctions and want a piece of the action. Just make sure you do your homework before submitting your bid.

The City of Detroit also has a bid website called. https://buildingdetroit.org. The deals are good, but enticingly good if you are a city worker and can acquire the properties for 1/2 price. It is always better to bid in an environment of many, many properties and a limited number of bidders rather than a limited number of properties offered and many bidders. Before finishing up this guide and starting on all the important things to do next, let me warn you about the things not to do.

CHAPTER 7

THE 10 BIGGEST MISTAKES INVESTORS MAKE AND HOW TO AVOID THEM

MISTAKES

GOOGLE MAP BIDDING.

Physically look at the properties before bidding or buying. If you live outside of the City, establish a relationship with someone in Detroit so that you will have boots on the ground. If you must rely on the internet do not use google maps because the pictures are old. If you have to bid without looking go to https://makeloveland.com for more current pictures. The best scenario could be to interview the occupant and talk your way inside.

"Uncapped assessments" or the assessed value rather than the taxable value. Most properties are not at full assessment. When property changes hands the assessment can go to the full assessed amount – we call it the uncapped value.

Make sure you review the property tax bills and even visit the assessor to assure that the assessment will not uncap and increase upon purchase or at least what that amount will be.

1. Investing Without Checking Title.
   If you do not want to pay for a title search, which might be impractical if you are underwriting several deals in a short time span, make sure you at least check the title history.

Go to Wayne County's land records website located at https://www.waynecountylandrecords.com/recorder/web and pay the few bucks for a search or go downtown to Wayne County Register of Deeds on the 7th floor located at 400 Monroe, Detroit Michigan 48226 and spend a day looking up deals.

2. Not Interviewing Current Occupant(s) Of The House.
   Before you buy you should know what the intentions of the occupants are; you might want to resell the house back to them.

3. Not Using Qualified Contractors.
   This is easy to fix. Make sure they get a permit and then you have the city inspectors as their supervisors. Do not always go for the cheapest bid - go for the best bid which includes the most qualified contractor.

4. Not Checking Building Safety Engineering (BSE)

Violations do not go away when a house is sold and usually neither do the fees. Make sure you spend a day checking out the violations before buying.

5. Investing Without Checking The Sewer Lines

Properties that have been sitting a long time can have sewer issues that may cost more than the house. It only costs about $175 to get a camera run through the sewer to determine if there are major problems. Houses next to large trees are a shoo-in for bad sewers.

6. Not Checking For The Water Bill

In June of each year the Detroit Water and Sewer service can transfer delinquent water bills to the County Property Tax bill. The problem is that the County Property Tax bill does not come out until December. If you bought property after June but before December, you could miss the whole thing. Make sure you always check property tax bills after you are the successful bidder so that you will not mistakenly pay the old water bill.

7. Buying Too Many Vacant Properties

This is a serious problem because of the carrying costs (i.e. taxes, insurance and security). Make sure you do a proforma... which can be found on www.stratheracademy.com. If you are going to buy a dozen houses, make sure the majority are occupied.

8. Buying In Areas That You Know Nothing About

Try buying where you either live, work, play or pray. You will be able to see the property weekly and know the lay of the land. If you are not sure about certain areas, contact Strather Academy at (313) 444-9691 or one of the references at the end of this book.

CHAPTER 8

DETROIT ZIP CODES ~
"HOT OR NOT."

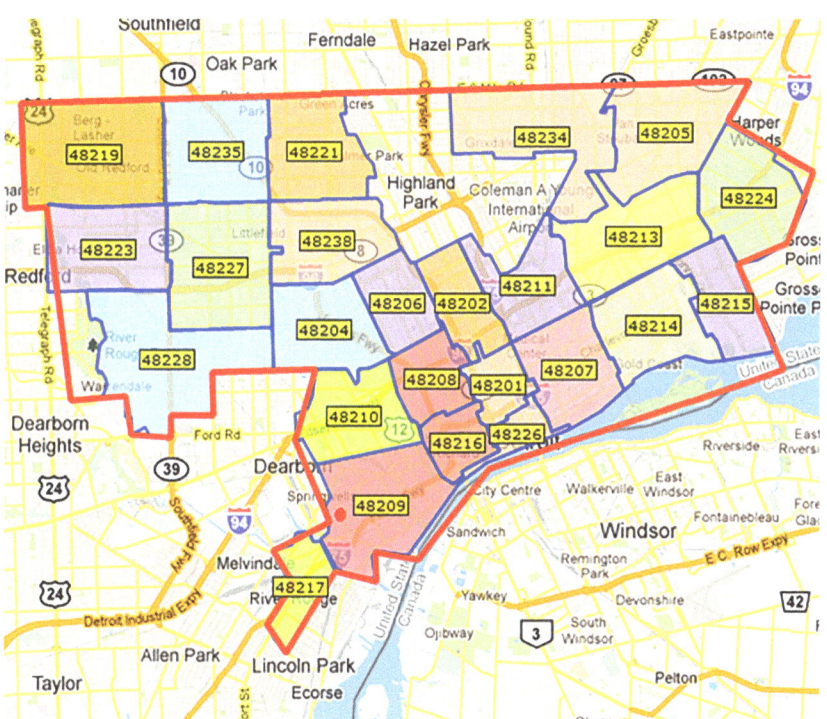

Disclaimer- Remember To Do Your Homework. Some Addresses Are Hotter Than Others In The Same ZIP Code.

RATING

A+

ZIP	Growth Category	Neighborhood
48201	**Hyper Growth**	**Brush Park, Medical Center, Midtown**

"HOTTEST ZIP CODE IN DETROIT."

- Woodward Ave / E Hancock St
- Woodward Ave / Putnam St
- Ecumenical Theological Seminary / Beaubien St
- Woodward Ave / W Forest Ave
- 3rd St / W Forest Ave

- Grand River Ave / Woodward Ave
- Michigan Ave / Trumbull St
- John C Lodge Fwy / Selden St
- Trumbull St / Ash St
- Woodward Ave / Henry St

RATING

A+

ZIP	Growth Category	Neighborhood
48202	Hyper Growth	Arden Park, Art Center, Cultural Center, New Center, NW Goldberg, Virginia Park, Wayne State

"BUY IF YOU CAN."

- Woodward Ave / Putnam St
- Oakland St / Custer St
- Woodward Ave / Owen St
- Woodward Ave / Hague St
- Wayne State U / Woodward Ave
- Trumbull St / Lincoln St
- Hamilton Ave / Lawrence St
- Woodward Ave / Edison St
- Clairmont St / 3rd St
- W Euclid St / Woodrow Wilson St
- Clairmont St / Byron St
- Woodward Ave / W Milwaukee St

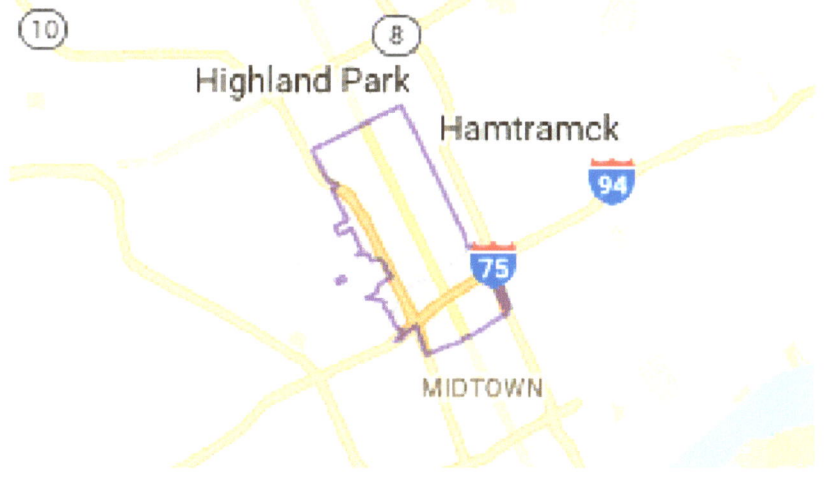

Rating

C+ - A+

ZIP	Growth Category	Neighborhood
48203	Gradual Growth	Chaldean Town, Highland Park, Palmer Park, Palmer Woods

"Stable Area In Palmer Woods."

- Orleans St / E 7 Mile Rd
- Emery St / Conant St
- E Remington St / Conant St
- E 7 Mile Rd / Omira St
- John R St / W 7 Mile Rd
- W 8 Mile Rd / Ralston St
- John R St / W 8 Mile Rd
- Conant St / Victoria St
- Conant St / Halleck St
- Woodward Ave / Pasadena St
- Linwood St / W McNichols Rd
- W 8 Mile Rd / Woodward Ave
- Pembroke Ave / Livernois Ave
- Woodward Ave / W 7 Mile Rd
- City Center
- Woodward Ave / Moss St
- Hamilton Ave / North St
- Hamilton Ave / Labelle St
- Oakland St / Massachusetts St
- Woodward Ave / Glendale St

RATING

B - C

ZIP	Growth Category	Neighborhood
48204	Selective Growth	Aviation Subdivision, Barton McFarland, Petoskey-Otsego, Russell Woods

"DEPRESSED AREAS."

- Broadstreet Ave / Cortland St
- Dexter Ave / Elmhurst St
- Grand River Ave / Joy Rd
- W Jeffries Fwy / Joy Rd
- W Jeffries Fwy / Seebaldt St
- Northfield St / Joy Rd
- Livernois Ave / Cortland St
- Fullerton St / Wyoming St
- Plymouth Rd / Manor St
- Wyoming St / Orangelawn St
- W Chicago / Livernois Ave
- Joy Rd / Livernois Ave
- W Chicago / Cloverlawn St
- Joy Rd / Oakman Blvd
- W Chicago / Wyoming St

RATING

C+

ZIP	Growth Category	Neighborhood
48205	Slow Growth	LaSalle College Park, Mohican Regent, Pulaski, Regent Park, Von Steuben

"Parts Have Challenged Areas. Buy Now."

- E 8 Mile Rd / Boulder St
- Gratiot Ave / Fairmount Dr
- Gratiot Ave / Maddelein St
- Chalmers St / Rochelle St
- Hayes St / Seymour St
- E 7 Mile Rd / Hayes St
- E 8 Mile Rd / Regent Dr
- E 8 Mile Rd / Schoenherr St
- E State Fair St / Schoenherr St

- E State Fair St / Hoyt St
- E 7 Mile Rd / Schoenherr St
- Greiner St / Schoenherr St
- Gratiot Ave / Rosemary
- Chalmers St / Flanders St
- Hayes St / Houston Whittier St
- Hoover St / Lappin St
- Gunston St / E McNichols Rd

RATING
A - B

ZIP	Growth Category	Neighborhood
48206	Increased Growth	Boston Edison, LaSalle Gardens, North End, Russell Woods, Virginia Park

"One Of The Hottest Areas To Buy Right Now"

- Dexter Ave / Elmhurst St
- Sacred Heart Major Seminary / Linwood St
- Chicago Blvd / La Salle Blvd
- La Salle Blvd / Tuxedo St
- Linwood St / Burlingame St
- Linwood St / Glendale St
- Glendale St / La Salle Blvd
- Woodrow Wilson St / Glendale St
- W Euclid St / Woodrow Wilson St
- Clairmont St / Byron St
- 14th St / W Euclid St
- Clairmont St / La Salle Blvd
- Linwood St / Clairmont St
- Linwood St / Lothrop St
- Grand River Ave / Joy Rd
- Bradford St / E McNichols Rd

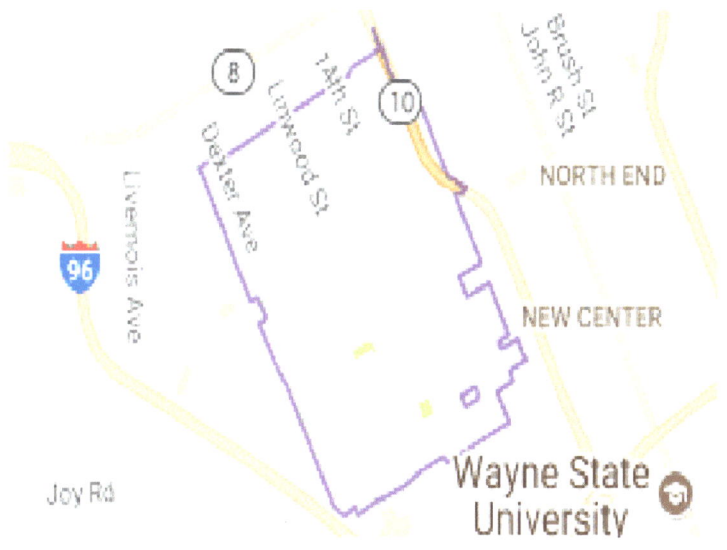

RATING
A - C+

ZIP	Growth Category	Neighborhood
48207	Increased Growth	Eastern Market, Elmwood Park, Forest Park, Island View, Lafayette Park, Rivertown

"HOT AREAS THAT WILL EXPAND IN RETAIL."

- Russell St / Wilkins St
- Muse St / Wayside Pl
- Gratiot Ave / Canton St
- Gratiot Ave / Helen St
- Mack Ave / Helen St
- Helen St / Kercheval St
- E Jefferson Ave / Mount Elliott St
- E Jefferson Ave / Saint Aubin St
- Mount Elliott St / Vernor Hwy
- Mount Elliott St / Gratiot Ave
- Saint Aubin St / Antietam Ave
- Gratiot Ave / Antietam Ave
- Chrysler Dr / E Larned St
- Mount Elliott St / E Forest Ave

RATING
A

ZIP	Growth Category	Neighborhood
48208	Increased Growth	Core City, Jeffries, NW Goldberg, Woodbridge

"GOOD AREA TO INVEST."

- Michigan Ave / Roosevelt St
- Trumbull St / Ash St
- Trumbull St / W Warren Ave
- Grand River Ave / 16th St
- W Warren Ave / Mckinley St
- W Jeffries Fwy / Vinewood St
- Grand River Ave / Lawton St
- Trumbull St / Lincoln St

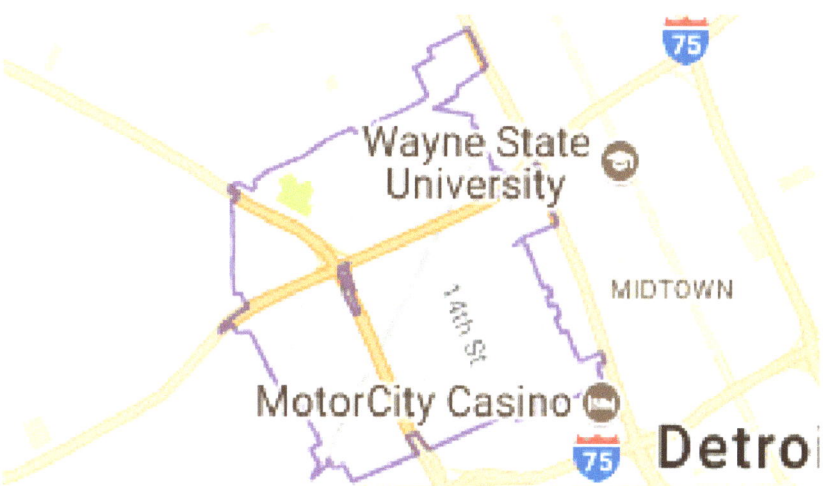

Rating
B

ZIP	Growth Category	Neighborhood
48209	Increased Growth	Carbon Works, Delray, Hubbard Farms, Springwells

"The Site Of The New Gordie Howe Bridge."

- Michigan Ave / Vinewood St
- Dragoon St / Vernor Hwy
- Vernor Hwy / Clark St
- Vinewood St / Vernor Hwy
- Livernois Ave / Lafayette Blvd
- Vernor Hwy / Dix St
- Dix St / Lonyo St
- Vernor Hwy / Springwells St
- Woodmere St / Rathbone St
- Delray
- Fort Wayne

RATING
B-

ZIP	Growth Category	Neighborhood
48210	Steady Growth	Clayton, Michigan Martin

"LOTS OF RENTAL PROPERTY. TIGHT KNIT COMMUNITIES."

- Livernois Ave / Tireman St
- Michigan Ave / Vinewood St
- Michigan Ave / Livernois Ave
- Michigan Ave / Cicotte St
- Michigan Ave / Lonyo St
- Lonyo St / McGraw St
- Central St / McGraw St
- Herbert St / 31st St
- Lonyo St / McGraw St
- Michigan Ave / Military St
- Proctor St / McGraw St
- Livernois Ave / McGraw St
- Tireman St / Rangoon St
- Tireman St / Colfax St
- McGraw St / W Warren Ave

RATING
B-

ZIP	Growth Category	Neighborhood
48211	Increased Growth	Pole Town, Milwaukee Junction

"INDUSTRIAL AREA."

- E Ferry St / Russell St
- Mount Elliott St / Dorothy St
- Van Dyke St / Lynch Rd
- Oakland St / Custer St
- Woodward Ave / Owen St
- Gratiot Ave / Canton St
- Farnsworth St / McDougall St
- Mount Elliott St / E Palmer St
- Caniff St / Conant St
- City Center

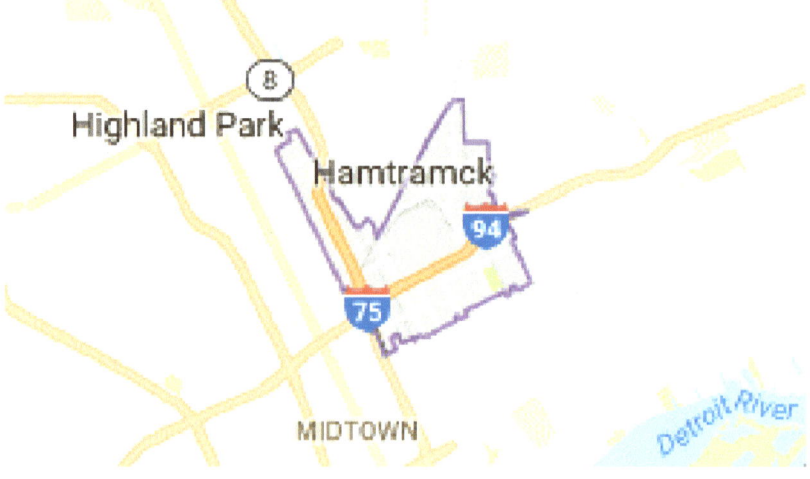

RATING
A - B

ZIP	Growth Category	Neighborhood
48212	Consistent	Hamtramck

"GOOD INCOME PROPERTY."

- Saint Aubin St / Holbrook St
- Van Dyke St / E 7 Mile Rd
- E Nevada St / Ryan Rd
- E 7 Mile Rd / Fleming St
- Conant St / E McNichols Rd
- Conant St / Victoria St
- Conant St / Halleck St
- Charles St / Mount Elliott St
- Van Dyke St / Lynch Rd
- Mound Rd / E McNichols Rd
- Conant St / Carpenter St
- Conner St / Joseph Campau St
- Caniff St / Chrysler Exp
- Conant St / Trowbridge St
- Caniff St / Conant St

RATING
B - C

ZIP	Growth Category	Neighborhood
48213	Slow Growth	Chandler Park, Gratiot Woods, Ravendale

"LOW VALUED HOUSES. NEEDS WORK."

- Gratiot Ave / Rosemary
- Chalmers St / Flanders St
- Hayes St / Houston Whittier St
- Chalmers St / Harper Ave
- Dickerson St / Harper Ave
- Harper Ave / Barrett St
- Grinnell / McClellan Ave
- Van Dyke St / E McNichols Rd
- French Rd / Harper Ave
- Van Dyke St / Lynch Rd
- Chalmers St / Southampton St
- Dickerson St / Frankfort St
- Gratiot Ave / Belvidere St
- Shoemaker St / Saint Jean St
- Gratiot Ave / Van Dyke

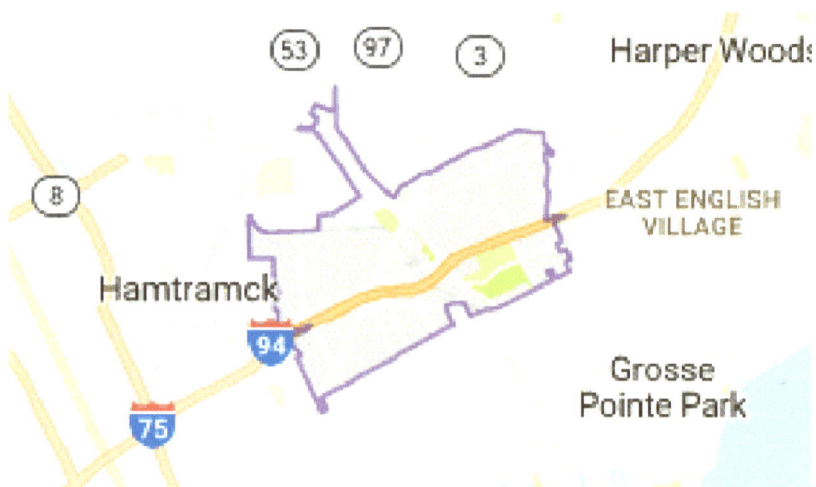

RATING
A - B

ZIP	Growth Category	Neighborhood
48214	Increased Growth	Conner Creek, (East) Indian Village, Gold Coast, Island View, Joseph Berry Subdivision, West Village

"ONE OF THE BEST AREAS. BUY, BUY, BUY."

- Conner St / Mack Ave
- Kercheval St / Cadillac Blvd
- E Jefferson Ave / Saint Jean St
- Mack Ave / Saint Jean St
- E Warren Ave / Saint Jean St
- Belvidere St / E Forest Ave
- E Forest Ave / Van Dyke St
- Mack Ave / Van Dyke St
- Field St / Kercheval St
- Seminole St / Kercheval St
- Crane St / Mack Ave
- E Jefferson Ave / Marquette Dr

RATING
A - B

ZIP	Growth Category	Neighborhood
48215	Increased Growth	Jefferson Chalmers, Marina District

"GOOD PROPERTY. HOLD THE LAND."

- Conner St / Mack Ave
- E Warren Ave / Gray St
- E Jefferson Ave / Alter Rd
- E Warren Ave / Chalmers St
- Kercheval St / Chalmers St
- Avondale St / Lakewood St
- Mack Ave / Chalmers St
- E Jefferson Ave / Saint Jean St

RATING
A - B

ZIP	Growth Category	Neighborhood
48216	Increased Growth	Corktown, Millenium Village, West Side Industrial

"GOOD INVESTMENT PROPERTY, A SLEEPER."

- W Jefferson Ave / Lafferty Vermont St
- Porter St / 24th St
- Trumbull St / Ash St
- Michigan Ave / Trumbull St
- Michigan Ave / Roosevelt St
- Michigan Ave / Vinewood St
- Vinewood St / Vernor Hwy

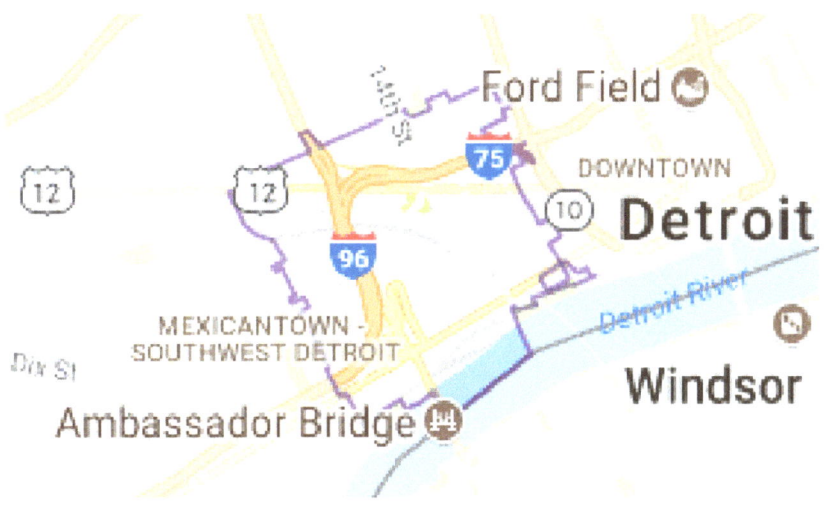

Rating

C - C+

ZIP	Growth Category	Neighborhood
48217	Slow Growth	Boynton, Oakwood Heights, Southwest Detroit

"Property Value Low. Industrial Area With Pollution."

- S Dix St / S Oakwood
- S Schaefer Hwy / S Fort St
- S Fort St / Visger St
- S Outer Drive / W Jefferson

RATING
B - B+

ZIP	Growth Category	Neighborhood
48219	Stable Growth	Berg Lahser, Five Points, North Rosedale Park, Old Redford, Riverdale, The Eye

"GOOD INCOME PROPERTY. SOME CHALLENGED AREAS."

- Greenview Ave / Faust Ave
- Huntington Rd / W 7 Mile Rd
- Vassar Ave / Evergreen Rd
- W 8 Mile Rd / Evergreen Rd
- W 8 Mile Rd / Chapel St
- Saint Martins Ave / Braile St
- Evergreen Rd / W 7 Mile Rd
- W 7 Mile Rd / Trinity St
- Five Points St / Santa Maria St
- W 7 Mile Rd / Berg Rd
- Lahser Rd / W 8 Mile Rd
- Verdun St / Shiawassee Dr
- Telegraph Rd / Frisbee St
- Florence St / Southfield Fwy
- W McNichols Rd / Ashton Ave
- Grand River Ave / W McNichols Rd
- Bramell St / W McNichols Rd
- W McNichols Rd / Fenton St

RATING
A - B

ZIP	Growth Category	Neighborhood
48221	Great Growth	Bagley, Green Acres, Martin Park, Pilgrim Village, Sherwood Forest, University District

"HOT AREAS."

- Linwood St / W McNichols Rd
- Puritan St / Linwood St
- Marygrove College / W McNichols Rd
- W McNichols Rd / Wyoming St
- Keeler Ave / James Couzens Fwy
- W 8 Mile Rd / Woodward Ave
- Pembroke Ave / Livernois Ave
- Woodward Ave / W 7 Mile Rd
- U of Detroit Mercy / W 7 Mile Rd
- Santa Maria St / Livernois Ave
- W 7 Mile Rd / Livernois Ave
- W 7 Mile Rd / Wyoming St
- Cambridge Ave / Wyoming St
- Pembroke Ave / San Juan Dr
- W 8 Mile Rd / San Juan Dr
- Norfolk St / Wyoming St

Rating
A - C+

ZIP	Growth Category	Neighborhood
48223	Good Solid Growth	North Rosedale Park, Rosedale

"Good Income Property."

- Oak
- Kendall St / Southfield Fwy
- Grand River Ave / Fenkell St
- Florence St / Southfield Fwy
- Evergreen Rd / Fenkell St
- Puritan St / Pierson St
- Fenkell St / Stout St
- Evergreen Rd / Schoolcraft
- Lyndon St / W Outer Dr
- Burt Rd / Fullerton St
- W Davison St / Appleton St
- Fenkell St / Bramell St
- Bramell St / W McNichols Rd
- W McNichols Rd / Fenton St

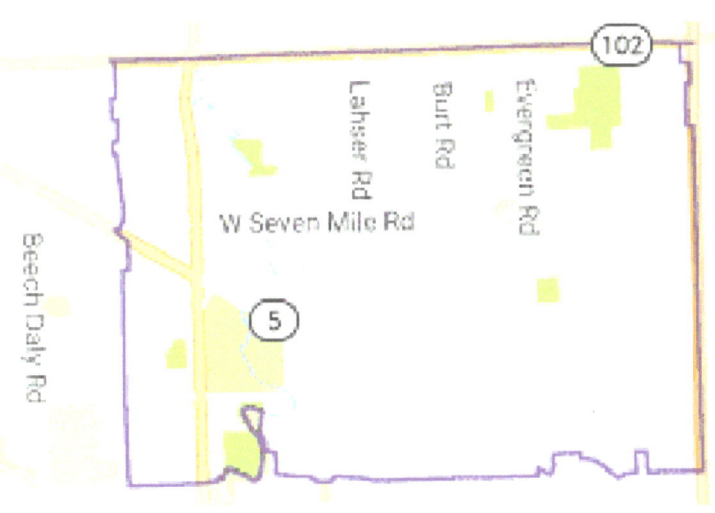

Rating
B - C+

ZIP	Growth Category	Neighborhood
48224	Solid Growth	East Village, Morningside, Yorkshire Park

"Good Income Property. Stable Neighborhood S of I-94."

- Balfour Rd / McCormick St
- Sanilac St / Casino St
- Morang Dr / Kelly Rd
- Grayton St / Beaconsfield St
- Wayburn St / Harper Ave
- Nottingham Rd / Whittier St
- Beaconsfield St / E Outer Dr
- Kingsville St / Harper Ave
- Kingsville St / Linville St
- E Warren Ave / Guilford St
- Cadieux Rd / E Warren Ave
- Haverhill St / E Warren Ave
- E Warren Ave / Balfour Rd
- Chalmers St / Southampton St

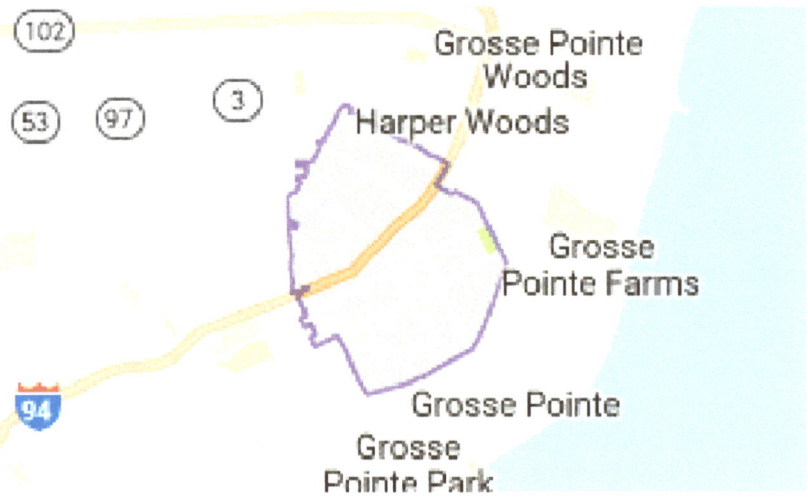

RATING

A+

ZIP	Growth Category	Neighborhood
48226	Incredible Growth	Downtown

"Retail and Sport."

- City Center
- Grand River Ave / Woodward Ave
- W Jefferson Ave / Woodward Ave
- Michigan Ave / Trumbull St

RATING
A - C

ZIP	Growth Category	Neighborhood
48227	Slow Growth	Belmont. Grandale, Grandmont, Grandmont #1, Green Briar, Littlefield

"Has Potential. Needs A Boost."

- Schaefer Hwy / Foley St
- Hubbell St / Plymouth Rd
- Puritan St / Schaefer Hwy
- Fenkell St / Schaefer Hwy
- Lyndon St / Ardmore St
- Pilgrim St / Archdale St
- Fenkell St / Forrer St
- Grand River Ave / Mettetal St
- Schoolcraft St / Schaefer Hwy
- Grand River Ave / Schoolcraft St
- Puritan St / Hubbell St
- Fenkell St / Greenfield Rd
- Grand River Ave / Southfield Fwy
- Schoolcraft St / Greenfield Rd
- Wadsworth St / Greenfield Rd
- Plymouth Rd / Greenfield Rd

Rating

B - C

ZIP	Growth Category	Neighborhood
48228	Mixed Growth	Fiskhorn, Franklin Park, Grandale, Herman Gardens, Warrendale

"Pockets Are Improving. Rental Property."

- W Chicago St / Schaefer Hwy
- W Chicago St / Hubbell St
- Joy Rd / Coyle St
- Joy Rd / Oakman Blvd
- W Chicago St / Greenfield Rd
- Joy Rd / Greenfield Rd
- Tireman St / Greenfield Rd
- W Warren Ave / Greenfield Rd
- Evergreen Ave / W Chicago St
- W Chicago St / Auburn St
- Paul St / Southfield Fwy
- W Warren Ave / Evergreen Ave
- Tireman St / Faust Ave
- Joy Rd / Grandville Ave
- Evergreen Ave / Joy Rd
- Joy Rd / Spinoza Dr
- Plymouth Rd / West Pkwy
- Evergreen Ave / Capitol St
- Evergreen Ave / Plymouth Rd
- Evergreen Ave / Elmira St
- Southfield Fwy / Plymouth Rd

Rating

B - B+

ZIP	Growth Category	Neighborhood
48235	Solid Growth	Belmont, Blackstone Park, Eight Mile Wyoming, Littlefield

"Should Make A Recovery. Good Income Property."

- W McNichols Rd / Schaefer Hwy
- W McNichols Rd / Greenfield Rd
- W 8 Mile Rd / Schaefer Hwy
- Cambridge Ave / Schaefer Hwy
- W 7 Mile Rd / Steel St
- Schaefer Hwy / W Outer Dr
- W 7 Mile Rd / Strathmoor St
- Greenfield Rd / Cambridge Ave
- Trojan St / Greenfield Rd
- Pembroke Ave / Greenfield Rd
- W 7 Mile Rd / Greenfield Rd
- Thatcher St / Greenfield Rd
- W McNichols Rd / Murray Hill St

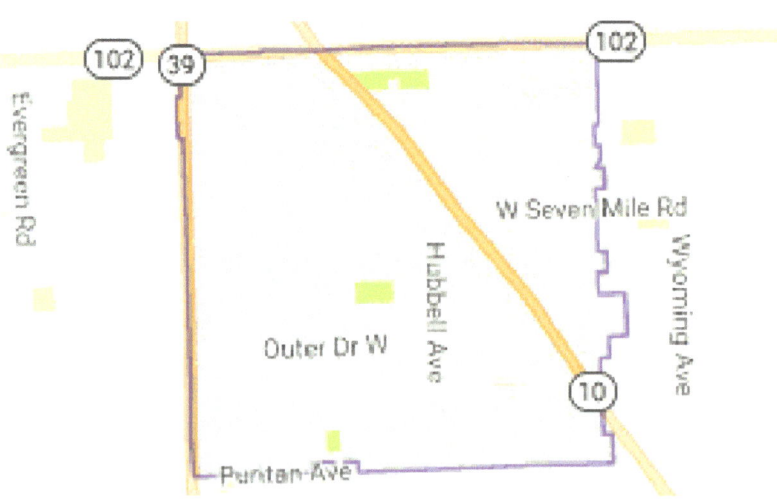

Rating

C

Zip	Growth Category	Neighborhood
48238	Increased Growth	**Fitzgerald, Harmony Village, Martin Park, Oakman Blvd, Pilgrim Village**

"Better Buy Now. Pockets Are Improving Fast."

- Linwood St / W McNichols Rd
- Puritan St / Linwood St
- Fenkell St / Linwood St
- Dexter Ave / Doris St
- Glendale St / Dexter Ave
- Linwood St / Glendale St
- Linwood St / Clements St
- Pasadena St / Rosa Parks Blvd
- Glendale St / La Salle Blvd
- Woodrow Wilson St / Glendale St
- Fullerton St / Wyoming St
- W McNichols Rd / Wyoming St
- Keeler Ave / John C Lodge Expy
- Fenkell St / Livernois Ave
- Livernois Ave / W Davison Ave
- Schoolcraft St / Wyoming St
- Fenkell St / Wyoming St
- Keeler Ave / James Couzens Fwy

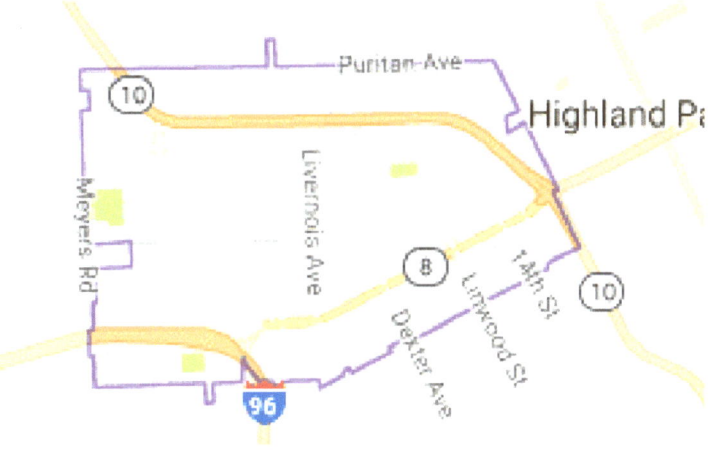

CHAPTER 9

PROFORMA

HOME STUDY COURSE BOOKS & FORMA

Get the Digital Home Study Course. This is a comprehensive six book course that will give you everything you need, starting with goal setting and ending with closing the transaction. It is our official textbook.

This course's content and structure was crafted and written in its entirety (a full **100%** for the mathematically inclined) from the lifetime experiences and trials that Herb Strather accepted, endured, learned and grew from.

BIDDING ON A PRAYER

A resource booklet to read **BEFORE** you bid at the Wayne County Property Tax Auction or the Wayne County Sheriff Sale. The book includes not only methodologies to insure success but also the **15 Items** not to do when Bidding at Auctions. There are also several 'proformas' ready to use to help you determine profits when you buy to flip, buy to hold or even buy to occupy.

ACQUISITION AND DEVELOPMENT COURSE

This is essentially a coaching course for those interested in Commercial Real Estate or those interested in accumulating a portfolio of real estate in the Detroit area. Here you will learn leveraging techniques to purchase property without investing the normal 20-25% down.

Class length is up to 32 hours and graduates are expected to close a deal within that time frame. 85% of the students have successfully acquired assets during the course. This class also covers how to restore your credit and set up a business line of credit. Students can automatically borrow up to $25,000 without any credit check to fund a savings account to use as collateral for a loan to repay the advance. You will learn the secrets to rapid rescoring and how to jump your credit score by as much as 100 points within a few months.

~ This course is also offered online in a streaming format via our website ~

REAL ESTATE 101

Here you learn the basics of everything from where to find properties, underwrite them, finance and the standard terminologies used so you can present yourself as a professional when dealing with the lenders. <u>This is an 8-week course</u>.

URBAN TURNAROUND & PROPERTY MANAGEMENT

Operating property in urban areas is not the same as suburban management. Learn what it takes to successfully manage the asset after you purchase it from a turnaround expert.

Final Wise Words to Investors

You do not have to try investing in the **"D"** alone. If you don't know trusted professionals that can help you acquire assets in Detroit. In Chapter 10 please find a list of our recommended sources.

CHAPTER 10

REFERENCES REVIEW

URBAN PROPERTY MANAGEMENT COMPANIES

Ivey Property Management
Address: 11000 W McNichols Rd, Detroit, MI 48221
Contact: Anniece Warren
Phone: (248) 419-1558

Bedrock (Downtown)
Address: 630 Woodward Ave, Detroit, MI 48226
Phone: (313) 373-8700
Website: bedrockdetroit.com

Urban Real Estate Brokers - Strather Associates
Address: 11000 W McNichols Rd, Detroit, MI 48221
Phone: (313) 444-9691

Bowers Realty
Address: 17277 W. 10 Mile Rd, Southfield, MI 48075
Contact: Darrlyn Bowers
Phone: (248) 557-1200

Century 21 Elegant Homes
Address: 26400 Lahser Road, Southfield, MI 48033
Phone: (248) 569-6633

Epic Realty
>Address: Northland Park Ct, Southfield, MI 48075
>
>Contacts: Wendy Hopkins (313) 399-2341, Susan Jones (313) 247-7740

MORTGAGE BROKERS

Quicken Loans (now Rocket Mortgage)
>Address: 1050 Woodward Avenue, Detroit, MI 48226
>
>Phone: (800) 226-6308
>
>Website: rocketmortgage.com

Hull Mortgage Company
>Address: 29226 Orchard Lake Rd, Farmington Hills, MI 48334
>
>Contact: Erika Shannon
>
>Phone: (248) 850-5080

REAL ESTATE LAWYERS

Harry Ellman, Esq.
>Phone: (248) 821-9995

Lewis & Munday
>Address: 1st National Building, Detroit, MI 48226
>
>Contact: Rueben A. Munday
>
>Phone: (313) 961-2500

Sullivan, Ward, Asher & Patton, PC
>Address: 1000 Maccabees Center, 25800 Northwestern Highway, Southfield, MI 48075
>
>Contact: William Freeman
>
>Phone: (248) 746-2733

Honigman Miller Schwartz and Cohn LLP

Address: 1st National Building, Detroit, MI 48226

Phone: (313) 466-7464

SERVICE PROVIDERS

Title Connect

Address: 28470 W. 13 Mile Road, Suite 325, Farmington Hills, MI 48334

Phone: (248) 642-3256

Email: info@title-connect.com

Website: title-connect.com

www.ingramcontent.com/pod-product-compliance
Lightning Source LLC
Chambersburg PA
CBHW040935030426
42337CB00006B/56